Wisdom Poems

A Compendium of 120 Poems on Contemporary life

Sriram Muthukrishnar

First published in 2020 by

Becomeshakespeare.com

One Point Six Technologies Pvt Ltd.

119-123, 1st Floor, Building J2, B - Wing, WadalaTruck
Terminal, Wadala East, Mumbai, Maharashtra, India,
400022.T:+91 8080226699

WORDIT ART FUND

This book has been partially funded by the Wordit Art Fund
Wordit Art Fund helps deserving authors publish
their work by providing monetary support
To apply for funding, please visit us at
www.BecomeShakespeare.com

ISBN - 978-81-948041-3-0

DEDICATION

"TO ALL
HARD WORKING
EMPLOYEES
IN
CORPORATES AND
THEIR FAMILIES"

ACKNOWLEDGMENTS

This book and my writing would not be possible, if not for my friend Mr. Varun Babar, who runs the Counter Point Music Academy in Pune. He trained me in observation skills that are needed for a writer/poet.

Rohan Patil and Shreyas from the publisher's team guided me towards a successful production. It was a tough time due to the pandemic but they endured to see this work happen.

Then to my wonderful family, who stood beside me like a rock, as I got into this venture, with strong faith and belief that I will write something useful for the benefit of the society.

My thanks to you readers, feel free to send your questions, comments and feedback to srirambm@gmail.com. I will be happy to interact with each one of you and take your views on how to improve this work.

AUTHOR'S NOTE

Life is a mixed bag of good and the bad. Many times, we are driven by the perceptions on what we see and hear but never have any idea on how the person feels inwards. This little poem book gives an insight on how I felt towards my life after long years of a high paying corporate job that the world saw as a good success to emulate. This book originated after my corporate stint of over 22 years and expresses my varied emotions on life.

Family, Health, Friends & Relatives and Integrity are the 4 pillars around which our non-working life revolves and it is towards these that we aspire for a good job, wealth and all the trappings of success to keep them happy. But when the subtle balance is lost between them, it is at first not noticeable but then eventually mushrooms into a big problem, dissatisfaction and life becomes totally meaningless. It was at this point in my life, I quit my job in an attempt to repair what was slowly breaking in my life. In search of a purpose, for happiness and fulfilment.

I have divided these poems or into various chapters for easy consumption as poems related to a particular aspect of life are all grouped under a particular heading.

There are 13 chapters that cover different aspects of life like Work, Friendship, Life & trends, Environment,

Nation, Creativity, Love, Motivation, Women, Technology and Philosophical poems.

You can read this in any order from anywhere in this book, but I suggest you read one complete chapter to take in my ideas and beliefs regarding that particular life aspect.

I consider the chapters on Work, Love and Philosophy as important and critical pieces to study. Other chapters throw light on aspects that we either take it for granted or ignore mostly. They are there to make you appreciate them and not miss out on the small things which in fact make a great deal of difference when it comes to real happiness.

Go ahead and read the poems. I hope you can resonate with me in some aspects and if you agree with me on where life has come to, please drop me a mail with your views. I will be glad to interact with you and I will appreciate and value your comments from the bottom of my heart.

Thank you very much.!

CONTENTS

1 WORK FOR BALANCE

"Work is a rubber ball. If you drop it, it will bounce back. The other four balls-- family, health, friends, integrity-- are made of glass. If you drop one of these, it will be irrevocably scuffed, nicked, perhaps even shattered."

—Gary Keller

Overworked?

I worked, worked, worked
And found myself in a trench
With no way out
The more I worked
The deeper the trench became
Then I figured, if I stopped the work
The trench stopped getting deeper
Now how to come out of the
Trench was a question that was
Deeper in my mind than the trench
The answer came when the family
Started filling the gaping hole
With love and hope
The trench slowly filled up with hope
That coming out was going to
Be easy, if you keep it steady.

Take a Break

Take a break when you can
Don't break your back
By carrying more than you can
We are not Donkeys
Trained to haul Laundry bags
For God's sake, we are humans
With dreams and aspirations
Break out of your comfort zone
Who knows you may like it?
Better to be out of a war zone
Then dread your day in
no Small tones.

Different Roles

Different roles dear folks
We have to do all the time
Some high some low
All in good Cheer
When people need you
Do not vanish
Your help is what they
Would cherish
Keep aside your bloated
Ego and do what it takes
To save the day.
At the End of the day, one needs
To be happy.
That does not Come a zappy.
Do not feed
Bitterness to show who is the boss
Everyone gets a time to shine
In their life. If you cannot wish
Them well, then just get out of
The way.

Conflicting Emotions

Conflicting emotions
Cause for a pause
To the crazy pace of life
Take a moment to survey
All without the commotion
There will emerge a clarity
As clear as the clean blue sky
Take a deep breath
Close your eyes, open
See the rainbow stunning
Conflicts purging
Only pure emotions sterling
To make your decision pending
As the Best of all per your circumstances

April Fool

Being somebody's tool
Is not an April's fool
It doesn't look cool
When the truth is out
So be careful of repercussions
of being a tool when sides
Change tools cringe
now you are at the receiving end
Of a plan that didn't go right
Because being a tool is never right.

Move On

Move on if you can't stay on
Do not lose your self-respect
With the Wolf's clan,
I suspect Find
the way, the universe will
Show the door when you really
Want a way, to move on
Let us go on to greater heights
With a smile on our face once
We decide to move on.

Corporate Mother's Day

Corporate wheels turn your heels
More you spin & more you turn
Money spins into coffers unknown

Stocks surge and markets splurge
Create wealth for people unknown
Alas but you don't get to see the
People you have known.

This Mother's Day
make a wish to know your folks
With memories more.

Different strokes
For different folks but all you need is
A mother's stroke, Every day.
Happy Mother's Day.

Rat Race

Rats run the rat race
Cats run the cat race
You can run whatever race you want

As long as you stay human
There is no human race
But humanity is at its stake

A race to the top is the cause
But no one knows when to stop
So, do we all become rats in the end

The pied piper will come along the
bend So be sure to end
The rat race before it has begun
Or
go to the same place in
Hamelin's end.

Dreamer

Every dreamer is looking for something
What he dreams is unfulfilled desires
Once obtained

It is no longer anything
He gets used and abused
looking for the one thing

He roams the day with glazed eyes
Hoping one day he will attain his thing
So, look for something worthwhile

So, look for something really worthwhile
To make the abuse justified
To feel the pain touched by time

Go and get your dream,
Go and get your dream
while you Still can
Every dreamer is looking
for something.

Spellbound

Spellbound at the seashore
Where he watched the waves
Swell mighty

He sucked in his
Breath and made a wish
To win this pageant manly

He Exercised with his dumbbell daily
To sculpt his body so nicely
His hope was to defeat everybody

With his body so mighty
That the oceans consider
It worthy to bless him with

A pearly smile that will be
the last mile for his Victory.

Family Lunch

On a Sunday afternoon, just after the sun
peaks, the human digestive system
Speaks to the brain

The stomach grumbles and the voice rumbles, is
lunch ready? Wife says Come on to the family table
Daughter says I want to eat a wee bit later

Son asks for a dessert first, mother says eat
Your vegetables first
Slurp, gulp, down dunk goes in the food

A plate full of *Roti or Puri,
Pulav & Dal, Subji and Chaas.
A rasagolla or ice cream
will put you in heaven

A nice doze after
adds a feather to your cap in heaven
Is this what home looks like?
If so, you don't have much of a worry
If not, you have the afternoon to think about it.

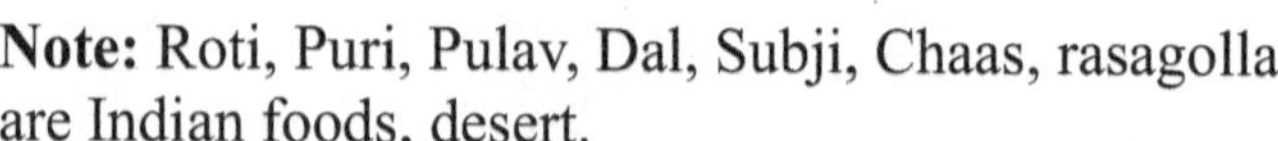

Note: Roti, Puri, Pulav, Dal, Subji, Chaas, rasagolla
are Indian foods, desert.

Globalization

Global business model
a havoc-wreaking model
In your personal life with travel,

Calls and escalations all together
In a nutshell Do we work all night?
and Still get beaten up
for getting up late

I see diabetes, hypertension, heart disease
at such a young age
What will happen when they really
age?

Money matters but cannot cause your
Health to be in tatters
See what really matters and do

The right choices for your daughters & sons
Lest they suffer the same global business model.

Vacation

Go, go get a vacation
For now, it is the celebration
Who knows what happens on deliberation?

Fate may Seek to cancel your vacation
Don't miss an opportunity for
Rejuvenation otherwise

it is Just a hallucination
This is all the medication
You need for your gratification

On a *WHO day, take a promise
That you will never miss a vacation
Now go and get your vacation

Note: WHO - World Health Organization

Corporate Job

There was a time when a corporate
job was worth a fight
It gave you status,
prestige, respectability,
all this with a good salary

Soon it became such a drag,
the more money you
got, you lost more time

Friends & Family You lost
Your happiness and purpose of life
Now you wonder
was all that worth a fight?
I would rather flee such
a worthless life

Remember friends, to fight or
flight is a choice you have to
do with conscience in your mind

2 FRIENDSHIP

"Friendship is born at that moment when one person says to another, 'What! You too? I thought I was the only one."

– C.S. Lewis

Friends are Made

Friends are forever
But to be made
They need to transform
Like diamonds

Amidst the noise & pressure
Intense heat & misery
Blooms the thickest of them

Like one without another
To share your lunch and
Laugh at your hair

To do late night movies
And comment on each other's flair
Rare indeed is a pair

Which indeed can achieve this fair
Hold on to this friend
Never let him or her go

Friendship Key

Whether you
are hot or not
The value
you bring
Is the
friendship key

Sound of Hope

The sound of hope
comes
In the form of your friend
When no one will dare
The friend will care

To give hope to things
That never might change

He may not use a bugle
But his voice is mighty sure

That is all the hope you will get
But sounds like it is a bet.

Crazy & Funny

Crazy as it gets
Funny as it goes
Someone trying to be runny

Without first being a bunny
Needs to know how to be funny
Should interact with many

Not so many
But a little many
Then he can be a bit funny
I think

Friendly Model

Such a friend is she
Who constructed a model?
With statistics

Gave it to me and said
Find out what will it do
I tried all possible options
And said it looks like
A predictor

What does it predict? said she
I said, thousands
of people Can fall
for you with a
70% probability.

Butterfly Seeks

Oh butterfly, butterfly, butterfly
What do you seek every day?
Is it love that you seek?
Is it friendship that you seek?

Love & Friendship I have not
But do not despair, I can give
You a nice plate of cheese

Full of lovely cheese for you to eat
It is called the mozzarella cheese

But if you give this cheese to
someone else You can earn
love or friendship as your hearts wish.

A b c d e f g, mozzarella cheese
has a lot of zee, now you can relax
every day   as, what you seek,
is always there.

Cuddles

Oh dearest, Your warmth
cuddles my friendly heart
when I see your walk,

I betray my thought
When I see your face
It makes me smile

When you see my face
It makes you laugh
Both we laugh not knowing

Who is laughing at what?

3 LIFE STYLE

"Find a purpose to serve, not a lifestyle to live."

-Criss Jami

Metro Man

Metro life, Metro Man
Is fast yet slow
We have a 1000cc Car

We drive at Snail's pace by far
We have *4g and 5g but
No time for *Parle-G with family
And friends

Our roads have tonnes of trash
But no one has any mood
To bother about the stench so rash

Life is fast for metro man
But speed kills as well as thrills
The deserted land

Parties and pubs abundant at hand
No wonder everyone likes the
Metro land

Note: 4g and 5g refers to cellular networks
Parle-G is a popular biscuit brand in India

Cloudy Morning

A cloudy morning
Said howdy to me
I was busy on my computer
Missed the courtesy

Ma computer froze
I logged back in
It said good morning
I could not ignore

I logged back into
my cloud account
Just then remembered
The cloudy morning

I shut down my computer
And went back to the morning

But by then it was afternoon
Told myself tomorrow morning
Then, I will catch up.

Easy & Crazy

Make it easy
People like it crazy

Use it lazy
Can't live without
It Daily

That's how you hook 'em
Daisy.

Just take it easy
That's life's policy

Stressed Times

In times of stress
All hands we must test

Is it from the west or the east?
We must check

Before we arrive at the result
To the watchers it is a game

To the players it is a shame
When death deals its blow

No one can stand in its way

4 LOVE

"To the world you may be one person, but to one person you are the world."

– Bill Wilson

Sweet Sixteen

Sixteen is sweet
The age of the teen
Only once it comes
Make it a poem

Anniversary

What is an anniversary?
if not a celebration of
another year
of love, of success,
of life-Well remembered and cherished

With near and dear
Even of a yester year
An opportunity to gather
Jest about and patter on

Simple vicissitudes of
Time
Then you have an
Anniversary, if not then
Just a memory.

Vanished

Here and there everywhere
I searched for you in my despair

But you vanished into thin air
And left me standing nowhere

I looked into your eyes once
To see the sparkle tense

Now I stare into the distance
To see if you can be found in any sense.

No Time

Absence of time
Is not an excuse fine

To not meet me in time
When we agreed for nine

Let this not chime
As an excuse every time

Don't ask if it is
Morning or Evening

This time I used a 24-hr clock
So, when I say 19

You know it this time
Absence is not excused

As you know the
Correct time

First Love

Words and Wordsworth
Was a mouthful to utter

Sometimes we make it
Together to get the
Right Words out to
of one another

Baby, baby just croon
Like Justin Bieber

And make your life easier
After all isn't it your first love?

Sing a Song

Sing a Song
Before dawn, that you sang
In your dream, Before she can
scream "Get up!

You idiot
This is not the
Bathroom"...

Yes, Maybe Love
Yes, maybe now
Who can speculate?

The way we go
It is not a rational thing
But more of a sudden fling

When an inner voice tells you
This is it! You simply have
To go for it.

Stay with me

You stayed by me
All my life

I ignored you
Most of the time
Life challenged you hard
You came over it sharp

Now you are a go-getter
I am still a fence sitter

No wonder you are called
The better half

I am yet to find my groove
You have nothing more to prove

But my love for you darling
Is nothing but pure.

Singing

Singing in the rain
He felt his life shine

In the early morning dew
The sunrise blazing through

Sparkling rivers and silver sands
Washing spoons in
Water fountains

His bliss, never at end
The rain showered its spell

The magic moments came together
When his girl said in a hum
She loved him really swell

Dearest

My dearest
You are my sweetest

Love your attitude
With gratitude

Love your pride
With my puffed-up heart

Love your courage
With my humblest part

I fold, my hands
To say you, thanks

But what really, I want
to do is open my arms

to take You into
my warmth!

Lonely Rose

A Rose lingers alone
With no one to care

It has thorns to keep
But no one to weep

The Rose smiles
Tells its friend

People only see thorns
But not my real form

A Rose I am
For only poets can see
How true "I am"

Mind Reader

I can read your mind
The way it waits for me
Time stands still
While waiting, patiently

I can read your heart
The way the sounds throb
Does it say my name?
It is always a game

When we are together
Time flies all together
Oh! what a fantasy
Your day with me

I can read your mind
Time stands still
Wake up from your dream
Don't make me scream

I can read your mind
Can you read my heart?

Bend Backwards

Bend as much as you can
Bend backwards or bend forward
To mend your relationship

The ship that sails your life
Amidst turbulent seas & roaring waves
Sails that flutter and hold your course

All because you could bend your hopes
Towards common shores
The lone star guides the great bear sights

Your bearings right
All because you could bend your rudder
Towards the distant lights

The morning star cries that you
Have reached your destination right

Because you were able to bend the
Sails of your life right.

Dancing in the Night

Tell me softly, Talk to me softly
Kill me softly but never leave Me

Softly, tender moments
Pass into strengthened memories
Kinder moments
call for musical Sorties

Dancing in the night
You can wrap into a tight
Embrace that kisses all night

Until the early morning dew,
Misty skies and chirping birds
Bring you to life

Filling me softly
Tell me softly, Talk to me softly

Taradiddle

She whispered into his ear,
Can we go the garden dear?
Yes, said he, into the lonely
    garden they went.

Now, what? said he,
let us taradiddle said she &
    giggled with glee.

So, he fibbed His heart,
    which she bought.
Now she sobbed,
"I should not have tara-diddled him"
What a sad day, if you go the
    taradiddle way.

Important Day

It was an important day
As I wait for him
Is he going to say?
The words, I cherish the most
I whisper to myself
Should I say "yes"
Should I say "no"
Say it that comes
To your heart

With these thoughts
I look at him
Deep into his eyes
Then I hold my breath
And close my eyes
Open my mouth

To feel his kiss
But all there was an
Emptiness, As I looked,
saw a running
Boy, scarred for life
the teenage years,
Full of twists for his
Sixteen years.

Sum of our Love

Sum of our love was lost
In a famous ship, a furious storm,
so frightening, made the ship
strike an iceberg
So appalling, that in a Matter of hours,
it sank, forlornly
She thought I drowned
I thought she will drown

But fate had it that
She fought for her life
While I watched her onto my death
We never had a chance to say

Till death does us apart
Years later when a diamond was found
Lost in the sea, an old lady
Found a story worth sharing

That made love to stand tall in its glory
Yes, it was a Titanic Story,
that still lingers in my heart
Not because of its tragedy
But because it is the Sum of our love.

Take me Home

Baby, Take me Home
I want to go home
Will you take me now?
I need you to caress me now
Whisper into my ear
Sweet nothings
That nobody will want to hear
I really want to go home, home
Baby, Baby take me home baby
Baby, Baby ride me home baby

I really want to really want to go home
Get on the bike now and hug my back
I will take you home make you warm
Trust me, Over a cup of coffee,
We will have our delight,
And sip it under the moonlight

When it's time to go,
You kiss me good,
I think, it is the good night
coming all again

Perfect Dream

I got a dream that you are my girl
When I wake up
you will not be there
you were my heart, I was your soul
that didn't part

I got a dream that you are my girl
In the morning, you got me coffee
And that was so rocking
Sugar and aroma, the spice

Heightened my senses and parted
Your lips. I woke up when we could
Have kissed. Baby it was
Just a dream, a dream that
I dream every perfect night

Take off the Mask

Take off the mask, so we can see the beauty
Take off the mask, so we can see the glory

With a smile on your face and love in your eyes,
you mesmerized me truly
Why do you need to hide the beauty?
speak with words of kindness,
that will remove my sadness
Seeing your beautiful face,
I took off my mask.

Will you take off yours?
So, we can get together lovely

Take off the mask and bask in the sunshine
Take off the mask and savour the wind
and you get fulfilled with
life, love, laughter and happiness.

That is why you need to take off the mask

5 CHILDHOOD

"We cannot always build the future for our youth, but

we can build our youth for the future."

— Franklin D. Roosevelt

The "Why" Poem

Why, Why, Why
Tell me why?
Asked the child
I don't know said the dad
But slyly he added
Ask your mom
Tell me why?
Asked the child
Why do you want to know?
Asked the mom
To learn said the child
Then ask your teacher
Mom said. The child
Now frustrated, he asked
the teacher, tell me why?
The teacher said it is
Not in the syllabus ask
Your dad. Now you
Know how it goes
Why nobody learns
What they should
Sad as it sounds
Tell me why? this happens
Asked the child

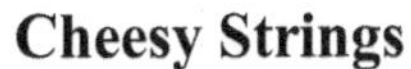

Cheesy Strings

String Cheese
String Cheese
I like you please
I like you please

Save your Flavour
For me to savour
A Chewy treat
So, sublime

I can pull a lot of strings
To get my string cheese.
String, String, string, String,
You ring, ring, ring, ring,

Pleasurable memories
Stringed through my mind
All because of a want
For a String.

Memory Lane

Down memory lane
When I ate ice cream
Behind a neem tree

Looked up at the sky
Saw two crows sitting
side by side
Chatting about the
Summer day

Of classes, tuition
And homework made
Exams done and free

To fly, my ice cream
Stick was only left

Ah! I said school memories
They were the most
Hilarious

What is in a Score?

This day you made us proud
You did your best and scored
what you could score

We feel happy with what you have scored
Life will not score you by your score
But by how you cared
for what you wrote

Learning happens by doing things
Experience things the way they are!

Rattled & Prattled

Why is this, why is that,
Why not this and that
Rattled and prattled
The little brats, that made my nerves
Stop in their tracks

But then I said, Curiosity killed the cat
To the brats who, Made pranks at me
For the cliché
But then I thought of a bright
idea called Encyclopaedia
Kids I said, do you want
to know w, w, w, w & h

They said what is that?
I said why, what, where, when
Is all explained with a "how"
in a book the "Encyclopaedia"

With the book in hand, the
Brats became geeks
Because now they know
All the w, w, w, w & h.

Holidays

It is the time of the year
For kids to do what they want to do
There were times when
We played cricket, football & Gilly
All in a local park

Now the trends have changed
WhatsApp, Facebook and Twitter
Snapchat, Instagram and what not
Is the new playground rather than the park

Going to the mall and paying a ransom
for an hour of play seems to be the norm

Does all this strike a chord with you?
Then think of playing humble games
like Hopping, jumping, skipping and
running

Hide & seek your friends at play so
That there is no need for mobile in games.
If you want to sit and play
chess and checkers are always there
Use your brain well at play and
see how easy to score marks with age.

Morals

There was a time
people had some morals
Nowadays people
are so immoral

Look at the CBSE paper leaks
Look at the banking scams
Look at the protests & riots

Across the land of ancient heroes
Who would all be ashamed now!
It is time to bring a change
So, bring a moral change
Students should read moral science
That was once an optional science

Pancha Tantra & Jataka tales
Tinkle with Supandi
That is how we learned our morals
I am just thinking out loud
If you agree, go make a change.

By Choice

A situation by choice is always
Better than a forced upon voice

To shine in your chosen path
With no one to break your walk

Know your interest in early years
So that you are not miserable in
Those crazy years- money, fame, status

Is what you desire or a basic *roti,
kappada & makkan will satisfy all
Your desires

Exercising such a choice
will it not be a dear, if it can bring cheer and
add to your good & happy years.

Note: Roti, Kappada & Makkan refers to food,
clothing and shelter in Hindi language

6 NATURE & CREATIVITY

"We don't inherit the earth from our ancestors, we

borrow it from our children."

- Native American proverb

Creative Design

A design so creative
Makes it a better narrative

Promises a visibility
That does not come easily

With so much to clutter
Very little to differ

Between trash and prose
No one cares to notice

The little misdemeanour
Design well with a meaning

So that the message may
Be clearer

Boundless Skies

Boundless skies
No end in sight
The horizon shows its might.
Nature's way, not all is Grey

Finds its sway, in the most
Thrilling Bays
Blooms of flowers
Removes gloom forever

Showers the receiver
With joy forever

Nature is joy, no need
To express it Coy

Enjoy it better if you
Know how to preserve it
Together

Smart is Dumb

When smart is dumb
A manuscript so profound

Finds no place around
People who care less
Or more of what needs
To be studied, amidst
The confusion of today
That exists in most literature
of late.

Write your manuscript
Nevertheless, for posterity
To discover Like the dead
poet's society, the future will
Find the manuscript to be
Smart for its time, then
Your thoughts survived time
A noble work to aim

Water is Divine

Water is divine, water is exquisite
Water is life said the thirsty man
Water can be mixed with various
Coloured things said the business man

The thirsty man got deceived by
The colour and thought it superior
To the colourless water.
The thirsty man thus bought
Cans & Cans of coloured water

The business man sucked gallons
And gallons of ground water
The ground cried; the earth quaked
The fields dried & wells emptied
Then realized the thirsty man
To quench his thirst, no colour was required

But to placate the business man
No amount of water is sufficient
Water is divine, water is exquisite
Water is life said the thirsty man

Nine Little Flamingos

A last one to last a long time
Said the poet who wanted to be
Nine little flamingos
Waited on the street
One by one
They fainted with the heat
Damn the heat said the mother flamingo
Down marched the elephants toot, toot, toot

Clown did come down and made the crowd hoot
Lions roared; tigers jumped
Fighters fought & flyers flew

It was all one great circus our
Lovable social media circus
Sunrise, moon rise, stars shine, heavens are fine
Whenever they rise people are just fine

But when they do have to set let us drop a
Tear, for the people who had
some interesting jeers, from queers, who
call themselves crazy ears.

Sky is a Canvas

The sky is a canvas holding precious stars
Nice to behold and dream about future years

Desires yet unfulfilled cloud my years
Yet tears don't come to relieve my fears Nice to
behold and dream about future years

The stars could not fulfil the promised desires
Yet tears don't come to relieve my fears
Making light my years of hard work

The stars could not fulfil the promised desires
So, they hid in shame behind the clouds

Making light my years of hard work
Was never in proper taste with the creator.

Twinkle Star

Twinkle, Twinkle little star
Now I wonder what you are
Up above the world so high
Like a spectre in the sky
You give me night mares
So scary, I am unable to
Say Daddy.

Daddy, Daddy
I am so frightened. Please
Make this spectre go away.
Spectre, spectre so scary
Give my Daddy back to me
Stars don't twinkle anymore
They just watch you go crazy.

Watched

Up above, in the heaven,
the stars watched over the humans
The humans mapped the sky
With many a clever device

The Stonehenge was one
With a mysterious design
Built to watch over the stars
By an ancient science

The Science was lost but
The Stonehenge remains
A silent testimony to the
wisdom of the past

Take a Bow

The curtains close and
the applause rose,
we take a bow with smiling faces

The show was a hit like
a Broadway musical
Classic was it but wasn't classical

The band played
the "chordettes", a musical Quartet

Mr. Sandman and Lollipop
brought in smiles and claps

Pom, pom, pom, pom,
this takes us further
into our musical journey
like an Elvis "capella"

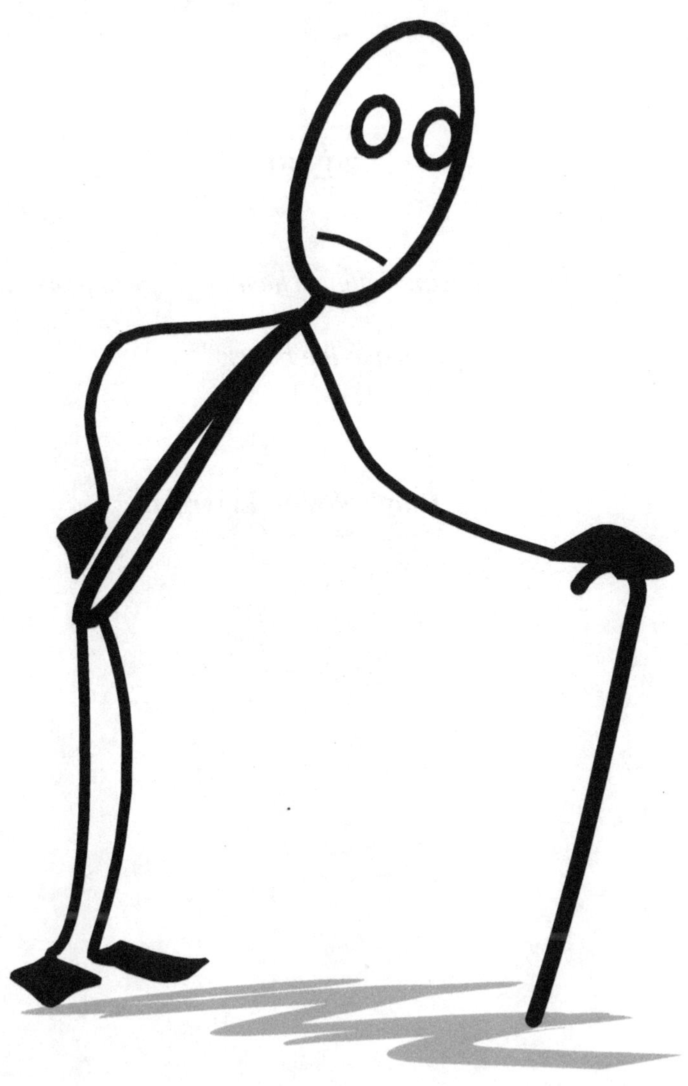

7 LIFE

"All life is an experiment. The more experiments you

make the better."

—Ralph Waldo Emerson

Countdown Counter

Age is nothing but a countdown counter
It counts your time to live
Live while the counter
Ticks below 50
Serve when the counter ticks below 60
Give when the counter ticks
Below 70
Surrender if you are lucky
And still got a ticking counter
After 70

Respectfully

Respect elders
Get blessed with wellness
Reap wisdom
Get Bestowed with virtues
Rest your sorrows
Get right solutions
Yours respectfully

Introspection

Looking back I saw
There was no need
But only to look forward
There were no bad
Decisions but good
Lessons and great
Teachers
Some good moments
To cherish and more
Moments to look forward
To
Look forward in anticipation
For there will always come
A day for introspection Other than this fine day
We call once a year
An anniversary to look back
But I look forward to this
Day ever year to look back
The way I lived and to
Make changes as I see fit
To make things better
And better
So I look forward
To looking back

Light Fell on Life

Light fell on life
When I stepped on
The gas to travel fast
To the hotel
As I hurry to meet my
Beau, I forget my coat
But was counting the
Days, till finally it
happened Today
As I introspect
I count the days
I was perfect
But it was none
So I think is it
What one needs to be
A perfect one?
Not necessarily
If I gave enough respect
To one and all
Then it would be
Just fine though less
Than perfect?

Paths

Take a different path
The one that is considered Hard
Great things take Time
For which patience is a dime
There is No shame in being poor
And no fame in being rich
Unless we do something Amiss
Take the path that takes
You out of slavery
That helps You live with dignity
Choose Wisely

Spider's Web

The spider's web was spun
For unsuspecting flies to come
The wait began
Till all the flies got trapped
Then it became food
She beckoned her children
To feast and have fun
The flies are coming again
The work must begin
Till then let's have some fun
Said the spider

Half & Full

Half is full
When your half-time
is done
Keep doing it
Till what is left
Is a big zero
Is this nuclear
Physics? No
Just your age
and ego's
Relationship
Is a half-time
Reaction too

Moving

Move a little
Shake a little
Do a lot
While smiling a lot
Do what is said
Cannot be done
Do more & more
Without getting bored
Keep moving to
Get going where
You want to go

Terrace

Terrace shields me from the Sun
As do the Tears cover me from pain
But there is no gain without the pain
The roof tops show the place
Where you mourn your shame
In silence we pray
For the pain to go away
Once the tears stop
You feel a relief so glad
That you want to dance
All round the terrace

Home & Heart

Home is where the heart is
Memories is where the art is
Writing happens when
There is an inspiration
Without any particular motivation
You write down your thoughts
At the place where you got your Shots
That is your writing place

Bad Guys

Bad guys are there
Every where
money can be made
They steal by deceit
Harmless they seem
But vicious is
Their realm
Be careful of where
You go they are
Capable of following
You through
Take a wise advice
Be thorough before
You throw your
Hard earned wealth
Into the villains Burrough

Blast from the Past

A blast from the past
That never let you pass
Through the travails of time
Is it a continuous thought?
Or a refusal to let go
The past continues so
The past is continuous
Then it becomes
Past continuous
Which is always a tense

Train

Train, Train
Train like an arrow
Go with the wind
Surprise your friend
Coal, steam, diesel or electric
You make it sound right
While the travellers have fun
Watching country sides
Never seen before
Bridges zipping by in a jiffy
Chatting up a storm
While drinking their Tea
Of stories long forgotten
Just to while away the time
Chug, chug, chug, chug
Toot, toot, toot, toot,
Train, Train, hoot your horn
I approach my farm
My station is here
So, I say good bye dear
You continue onwards
Take care dear

Very Stuck

Stuck in a dark sludge
Pretty feet got mired in sand
So coloured that reminds one
Of tough times covered and
Uncovered by the tides at Its will.
Thus so humbled
I look at the oceans and ask
Are you mean or nice?
Replied the ocean with
A pearly spray that uncovered my
Legs and left it clear
Do I have to figure this out?
I suppose so
Nice or not Seems to depend on how long
I stick my feet in the sand
Go figure out

Bitter Sweet

Yesterday was bitter
Today is a bit sweeter
Tomorrow will be better
Live a life bitter sweet
The bitter makes the sweet
Better. But too much sweet
Just makes you sicker
Take this with a pinch
of salt and the bitter
May just get better
So will you be a trend setter?
Bitter sweet Bitter sweet

Sweet Home

I wish every road will take me home
I am eager to see my home

The place I grew up, the place I had
Multiple Memories of me making merry with many

Enjoying holidays with so many a book a day
Sleepy days and sleepless nights
Endless cycling days with friends, fun & frolicking
away A picnic to the beach and football in the
hot sun never failed to make my day
Moms sweets and candy got us to pass every day
A sweet home is always the best place to be
as there is no place like home

8 OUR ENVIRONMENT

"The Earth is what we all have in common."

—Wendell Berry

Tree's Fault?

When heavens pour
It is a mercy, it is a curse
To those who lack, it is a mercy
To those who have, it is a curse
Is it the Cloud's fault or the
Winds fault? The fault is
Neither but with us. Those
Who cut the trees got the curse
Those who saved the trees got
Blessed. The saving action
Blessed and the cutting action
Brought the floods. To cut or
To save, we decide and so
We enjoy the results as per
It's seed.

Summer's Dream

Summer is here
It is indeed hot in here
So what do I do dear
Switch on the AC clear
But I fear for the environment
What do you fear
The ozone hole dear
How big is it?
I don't know but big enough
To bring a bomb cyclone dear
Ah. Then let us go natural here
I open the windows
Open the curtains
Switch on an air cooler
It feels so better dear
I wish I had done this earlier
Never too late this year
Try it if you care for the Earth dear

Bicycle

Two is company
Four is a crowd
For a cycle that is small
A crowd that it still carries for all
Time will tell
The pace of change
Did Nanos change the world
But sparrows save the world
Ye man, go back to nature
Be mature to realize that
It is the only way, only way, only way
Thus spoke the bicycle to the crowd

Weatherman's Rain

The weatherman said it will rain
I flipped another channel
There too it said the same
I danced with joy
As I saw a decoy
To take a day off
So I took a good book from
My shelf in the nook
Made myself a steaming coffee
Sipped it softly
Dipped my hand into the crispy *pakoda
Then waited for it to rain
But alas the weatherman was wrong
And he was gone
I was trapped in the channel's tryst
With weather gone amiss
So I caught a bus, on my way
To work, thinking of another decoy
With pakoda & coffee for my
Boss who is always cross

Note: Pakoda is a crispy deepfried Indian Snack

Mosquito Mess

Drenching rains the monsoon brings
Thrills everyone and gives them wings
Fills every pond, canal well & puddle

But With it comes the hoards & hoards
of mosquito trouble

Malaria, Dengue and other deadly diseases could tryst
at your place If not careful in keeping them at bay

Do not let water to stagnate in puddles
That can cause mosquitoes to reproduce in doubles

A wee bit of planning can save a hell a lot of trouble

For it is the mosquito season starting in a trifle

9 NATION

"A nation that cannot control its borders is not a nation."

— Ronald Reagan

Eagles Dare

Where eagles dare
Our soldiers return everyday
So that the homecoming
Of an Indian is safer
In every way

Then is it not our job to
Return the favour in some way?

Come to think of it
Yes we can, if we vote
Responsibly

Some say Nothing can be changed
But those days are long
Gone past
Now the power Is in your hands and
The wisdom to not fall in paltry corruption

Make use of it In such a
way that you can
Return the favour in a big way

Troop Movements

Shore up troops
Battle lines arraigned

Preparations are on
Both sides are gone
Into deep discussions
With high command

To decide who is right
I say God in his might
Will decide what is correct

While all others
Have to play the role
They are ordained
In this play

Shall we pray for all
That this does not go on
for long

Say no to war
There is No other
door to knock

Blow the whistle

A starry night is not
Good for dreams

I would prefer a Dark night theme
For a good dream I would see Batman,
Robin and Green lantern
But hope not the weasley
Spidey

All marvelous men and
Super heroes, did
They dream up their fate?

Let me ask In my dream
They are heroes
Who do the right things

Blow the whistle, When bad people
Do wrong things And that is how

They became HEROES not just
In my dream

March Ahead

A foot, a step, one at a time
Makes you walk across the
Sands of time

Left first Right next march past the
Flagpole

Footsteps thud
The band blows, onlookers
Cheer footsteps you hear
Children revel Seargents
Whistle, floats go by with
Dancers talent show

Thus The states unite every year
With a show that thrills
Everyone's minds

The Beggar

Ugly smiles, crony look
Dirty clothes and a crooked stance
Haughty looks from passers by
Weary from the days pain

The beggar looks at you again
Will you or won't you
Pay him a dime

Is a game you can play every day
But the day you make his day a bright

The ugly smile flashes a glimpse
Of stain
He salutes you for this
Paltry sum to make you feel so grand again

Adulteration

Purity is a rarity these days
With food adulterated in all its forms
White stands for purity

It reminds one of peace & tranquility
White stands for purity

It reminds one of widows too
White stands for cleanliness

Cleanliness of thoughts, deeds & actions
White stands for morality
The standards of conduct in business & life
White stands for love

A mother's love when her breasts overflowed
With the milk of love for her offspring
Such a great colour is white

May it be given its due right
Happy world milk day
May it not be altered anyway

Rainy Weather

What to do if it rains
Is it a rhetorical question?
When it rains
There are no gains
Our work is hampered
Plans are scampered
Roads are full of filth
Traffic becomes a terrific itch
Power trips with a lengthy shower
Electric poles totter & topple
Man holes become killer holes
For the poor man on the road
We can clear the ditches
To save our homes from
The Water syndrome
Make our lakes, ponds & rivers
Richer by keeping clean
Our roads & drains is what we need to do
If it rains

Terror or Error

All terror is just error
Could have been avoided if just clever
Power with error is the reason for terror
Trade the power with Gods merciful shower

An eye for an eye and an arm for an arm is
not the best trade in this business
But the right to practice one's faith without distress
is the measure of our success

Peace will be upon this earth as promised
by the prophet, if only we can trade the
errors with forgiveness

Stand Alone

It is difficult to stand alone
Unless you are built to fight alone
Lest Go Draw your muskets
To fight the corrupt misfits

Prose & Poetry are the two
Musketeers, that puts
Fear unto the power of the word

Godspeed, the 3rd Musketeer
To shine in his mission
to save the nation,
so say the 2 musketeers

Cowards

With arrogance and malice as his play
The coward makes hay with his prey
When confronted with courage

The coward shows his crying face
So toxic is he that he fumes hurt
That mars trust in humanity

But don't sway to this cowardice
For there is a price to pay

Either in heaven or hell we know not
But before he parts from this
Wonderful Earth any day

10 **MOTIVATION**

"Our greatest glory is not in never falling, but in

rising every time we fall."

— **Confucius**

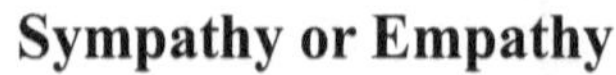

Sympathy or Empathy

I neither need sympathy
nor charity
But empathy that seeks to
Understand what is ethical
And what is not
Freedom to choose
A path that is moral
Over immoral paths
That hurts the heart
Don't misuse your freedom
Nor your power
Of words and dictum
To hurt another
Over paltry rights and
wrongs which you yourself
Are a culprit to many times
To all dictators
You will face the same end
As of all others before you
Mend your ways or
Be taught a lesson
That you will not forget
Daring people to Target
Is the most foolish thing
To do, in the current climate

Tomorrow

Tomorrow never comes
Use today for your ends
Live life as it comes
Because tomorrow never
comes

Tomorrow brings hope
So that today you can live
Use tomorrow in a positive way
So that today was better than yesterday

Dead Poet

A dead poet is of no use to the society
So seize the day like how cats seize
Their prey

To write more of your precious thought treasures
with dexterity

May it find its heyday in posterity
Good enough to form a dead poet's
society

A cat is said to have 9 lives and a poet can have 99
lives, so seize the day and pave the way for
future generations to say I read *"your name"

Note: "Your Name" seriously reader, go ahead and
start writing your own poetic creations.

11 WOMEN

"Any woman who understands the problems of running a home will be nearer to understanding the problems of running a country."

– Margaret Thatcher

Keep your Distance

Keep a distance
Irrespective of resistance
Keep an eye
In spite of Denial
Keep a Pen
As a safety device
Keep looking
Behind the mirror
The Man in the front
May not keep his promise

Smell of Gold

The smell of Gold is wafting
in the air Just like marigolds
in the lair
of the fancy girl's hair

Ornaments sparkle sometimes
Dazzle but lose out to the
Pearls on the prettiest face

Oh between the Jewels, pearls
And Marigolds, what makes
Her pretty? Said the man
It is always the smell of
marigolds Mam

Lady of the House

The lady of the house
Sat alone and wept

The children have flown the nest
After the wedding at its best

It feels lonely and desolate
Will anyone take care of me
In the nest, she thought

The food is less but the love is
More
She wants to share but
There is no one any more

Will you be my guest she asked?
I said with pleasure

I am a brother at his best
Always the Safest bet

12 TECHNOLOGY

"It has become appallingly obvious that our technology has exceeded our humanity."

–Albert Einstein

of Asking

Ask it like a pro?
What you may Ask

The questions said I

Why not seek, said he
If I don't know I seek
Then what said he I google

If not then Duck Duck go said I

What about yahoo?

Then it struck a bell bing!
So now we ask Bing
For all things pro
Look it up in a Bing

Smart Phone

I looked at my smart phone
I wished it was gone
To the era of trunk calls
And postal letters
Life moved at snail's pace
That suited my ways
Nowadays we got dumb
The phones got smart
They harass you nonstop
With their notification & calls
Enough is Enough said I
They continued their mutiny
When they said
You have 1000
unread notifications

Distance

Distance to go, Distance to come
Makes double the distance
Every day to cover, Is this really clever

When technology is so near
To travel to work, Like slaves of yesteryear

The fuel price has risen
Incrementally like a poison
Stealing your Cash
That could have paid your
Kids summer class

No more distance to go
No more distance to come
Just make a decision
To work from home

13 PHILOSPOPHY

"The unexamined life is not worth living"

– Socrates.

Guru

A *Guru is the divine in mortal form.

The one and only one, who has the ability
to deliver you from all kinds of miseries
born of this world due to birth, death,
old age and disease.

Faith and surrender are the 2 key ingredients
that can make one successful under a
Guru's tutelage

The greatest of such Guru's was *Sripada
*Ramanujacharya who
hails from the small yet holy town of
*Sriperambudhur

Breath

Breath is the sign of life
Important yet ignored
Taken for granted

Until you catch a cold
And get a nose block
Will show you how long
You can sustain
Without medication

Watch your breath carefully
Magic happens every moment
You inhale and exhale

That connects you with powers unknown
that makes your
Life tick tock, like your heart beat
Breath-is the essence of life

Helping Hands

Help those ask
Help those who may not ask
Do not let things to pass
If it is in your power
To help people with a past
True colours often show
When you seek genuine help
People take credit
For things not done

Such is Human nature
That brother murders brother
In the name of God Still you must help
One another
To recognize these follies
For we are born
Unfortunately, Human

Gold Inspection

Will Gold inspect Gold for quality or perfection?
Will face become mirror to see its own reflection?

Will Earth transform to Crops without
Sun's intervention?

When the seed is seen, the tree is hidden
When the tree is seen the seed is implied

Can the student become the
master to learn teaching?

Writing is like the seed in you that
blossoms on reading

Keep questioning, the questions
Until all questions are tested for reason

You will find joy in the questions
and pleasure in the answers

Fate Mate

Fate is your ideal mate
Which follows you across
All weather at its wake

To brave the Storm that
will eventually come
when rough weather
Hits, the rougher's stick

Make the days count for
It will go just like it came
In a whiff of smoke

Fate Falters to those who
Hope with God as the
One they trust
In whose hands they rest
All others can only try
Their best to follow fate
At it's behest

Destiny Takes

Your destiny is yours to make
If you got what it takes

To explore the unknown
Down deep in the depths
Or high up in the mountains

Till your soul recognizes
Your destiny

It feels like A satiated tummy that gives
You a tingling bell that
You have found what you
Went to look for

Rainbow

I saw the rainbow and ran after it
Because someone said there is a pot
Of gold at the origin

Alas after I reached the spot
There was no pot of Gold but just
A scarecrow

It stared at me and I stared back.
Now that you ran so long after
Fool's gold, do you know the
Way back, it asked

I said, I don't know the way but
I will run back the same way following
The Rainbow

I turned back to catch the rainbow
But it vanished into thin air
While the scarecrow laughed
It's head off
Sheep Grazing
A Sheep grazing yonder
Felt unsatisfied with his feed

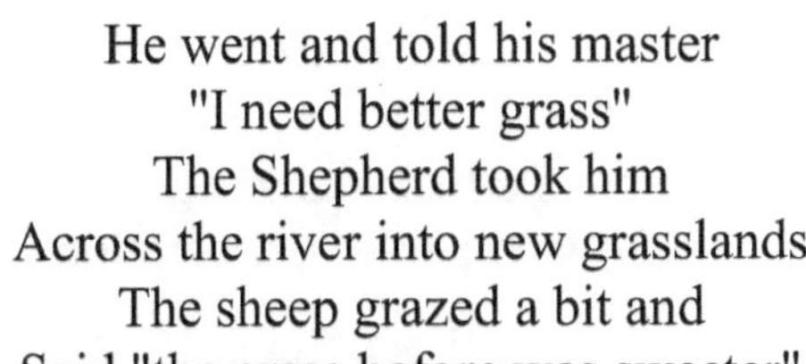

He went and told his master
"I need better grass"
The Shepherd took him
Across the river into new grasslands
The sheep grazed a bit and
Said "the grass before was sweeter"

"That my dear", said the Shepherd
"Is nothing but the Theory of Relativity
In action"

The grass is always greener on the other side
Learn to live with it, said the Shepherd

of Creation

Perhaps we create
To later revisit our creation

To see how much of it
Holds true with the passing
Annals of time

For there is Joy in returning, to be amazed,
To be dazzled and then ponder
To find that what really has
Changed is you and you alone

Inspired by Art

He inspired
We learned
He wrote
We read
He Shared
We laughed
Now he yearns
Let us not pretend
Presence is not missed
If his legacy is kissed
Stay true to the art
It will serve you
For life

Kill your greed

Kill your greed and earn some peace
Then Smile at ease so it feels
Lighter than cheese

Say please & thank you
To your elders please and
Earn their respect & blessings
With ease

Lose your attitude and Show some
gratitude See luck and fortune
Flow in with fortitude

Always think positive thoughts
So that there is no room for
Negative spots

Forgive people for all faults done
Let God be the judge of all
Things done

Make it a point To do this right and see
Your life transform bright

Shadows

Shadows are the windows
To the soul that needs awakening

The light of the soul is obstructed
By the dark thoughts like
Anger, Envy & Enmity we behold

The shadow appears as long as
There is light

Despair not still There is twilight

Let not the darkness become
An eclipse, but instead let us travel
Into a place, where there is only
Light

Life's Secret

The secret to writing is in reading
The secret to reading is in hearing
The secret to hearing is in silence
The secret to silence is in stillness
The secret to stillness is in meditation
The secret to meditation is in mantra
The secret to mantra is in Aum
The secret to Aum is in breath
The inhaled breath is *'so'
The exalted breath is *'ham'
The secret to this breath is in observation
The secret to this observation is your nose
I humbly prostate to this all pervading
Aum, to teach me these secrets

Note: 'So Ham' is the sound of breath in Indian Yogic System

A tragic rhapsody

Birth, death, old age & disease are the Four,
That takes its miserable toll
On this noble earth
Irrespective of one's birth

So said the Prince
who fled his princely life
To think For the good of mankind

Death said he is just a transmigration
of The soul immortal from body to body

Understand this magic to be free
lest A tragic rhapsody of the mind
a trillion deaths that nobody Can fight

Know what you are so that you
can become THAT once for all

The veil has to be removed,
so that The light can illumine
The way To see how
beautiful a soul you are

Ode to the Great

A great wizard was he,
who killed demons so great
Even when he was small,
was he a threat
lifted a hill with his little finger
to save the cows
from distressing showers
Seven days did he stand
with no help at hand
when the showers did end,
the ruler of heaven wept
with Love for the little
child born in a prison
He grew up to be a yadava king
and ruled with dignity
he took care of his friends smilingly
when brothers took to arms,
he watched them without alarm

When the mighty archer
surrendered to him in the
gory battlefield of brothers

He took his precious time
to talk about the affairs
of the Universe
The wizard spoke the magic words,
that brought solace to the archer king

The king took his bow
and vowed to fight till the end.
Do you want to know?
what the wizard said,
then read the ode to the great

Do you want to know?
what the wizard said
Then read the ode to the great

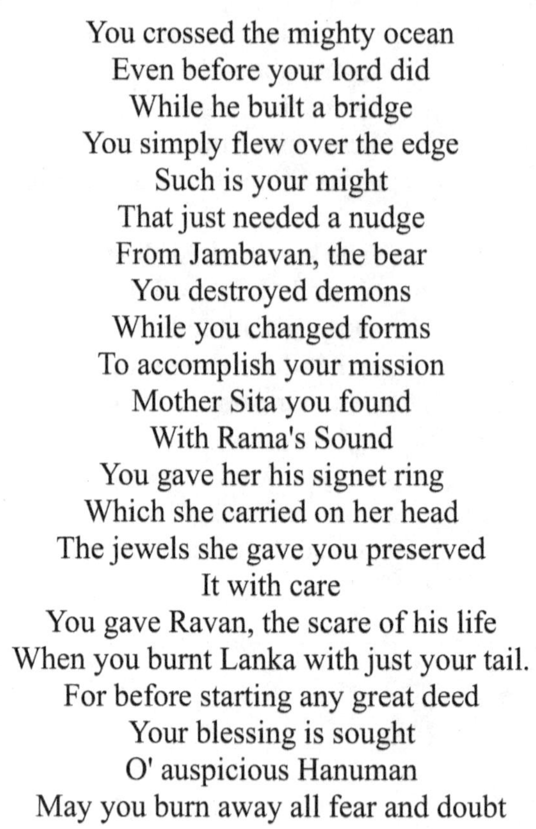

You crossed the mighty ocean
Even before your lord did
While he built a bridge
You simply flew over the edge
Such is your might
That just needed a nudge
From Jambavan, the bear
You destroyed demons
While you changed forms
To accomplish your mission
Mother Sita you found
With Rama's Sound
You gave her his signet ring
Which she carried on her head
The jewels she gave you preserved
It with care
You gave Ravan, the scare of his life
When you burnt Lanka with just your tail.
For before starting any great deed
Your blessing is sought
O' auspicious Hanuman
May you burn away all fear and doubt

Jai Hanuman

ABOUT THE AUTHOR

Sriram Muthukrishnan, a former IT executive by profession, has worked for the best of Fortune 500 organizations across the globe in his 20+ years strong Quality Engineering and Information Technology career.

After being a U.S resident on a h1b, Sriram returned back to his motherland in 2001, just before the 911 crisis that hit New York. He worked in various reputed IT MNC's like TCS, Cognizant and HCL technologies and rose up to managing large offshore delivery teams for blue chip clients.

Though being a top performer in his job, he dreamt of a life where he can experience true freedom and happiness - which did not seem to be coming from the tight demands on time that were made on him due to the nature of his Job and globalized Industry.

During his enriched career, he saw that most of the people around him are stuck in the same rat race, facing similar challenges, undergoing the same frustration and stress, and having no clue of how to come out of this meaningless loop in order to live their true dreams. Most of them had no idea whether a better life is even feasible.

After a year successful career with IT, he decided to reboot his career by switching to entrepreneurship. After the teething struggles, he along with partners founded a SaaS Startup in the legal services niche. While circumstances made him exit this venture, he started his second venture in Overseas Education Consulting.

Hailing from a middle class family in Chennai, India and having the exposure and experience to stay in varied societies and religions across the globe, he has been able to capture the pulse of the people and what gives true happiness to them.

A computer science Engineer by training, turned Author, Sriram Muthukrishnan has penned his experiences and emotions in Poetry form to bring you Wisdom Poems, a summum bonum of his variegated views on life. He stays true to his committed goals of helping others see *"How things really are"*, so that everyone can identify areas in their life that needs enrichment and fulfillment.